who?

Albert Einstein

알베르트 아인슈타인

Biography Comic
who? ⑫ Albert Einstein

초판 1쇄 인쇄 2011년 4월 8일
초판 8쇄 발행 2013년 4월 10일

지은이 강민희
그린이 스튜디오 청비
번역 자넷 재완 신
감수 김수희
펴낸이 김선식

Brand Creative Story Team 박효영, 김선영, 이유미, 전해인
Creative Management Team 김성자, 송현주, 권송이, 김민아, 윤이경, 한선미
Creative Marketing Dept. 이주화, 원종필, 백미숙
　　　　　Online Marketing Team 김선준, 박혜원, 전아름
　　　　　Communication Team 서선행
　　　　　Contents Rights Team 김미영

출판등록 2005년 12월 23일 제313-2005-00277호.
주소 경기도 파주시 교하읍 문발리 529-2 3층, 4층
전화 02-702-1724(기획편집) 02-703-1725(마케팅) 02-704-1724(경영지원)
팩스 02-703-2219
이메일 dasanbooks@hanmail.net
홈페이지 www.dasanbooks.com
출판등록 2005년 12월 23일 제313-2005-00277호

필름 출력 스크린그래픽센타 **종이** 월드페이퍼(주) **인쇄·제본** (주)현문

ISBN 978-89-6370-440-1 14740
SET 978-89-6370-438-8

who?

Albert Einstein
알베르트 아인슈타인

글 **안형모** | 그림 **스튜디오 청비** | 번역 **자넷 재완 신** | 감수 **김수희**

Dasan Kid

Albert Einstein

Physicist, March 14, 1879 ~ April 18, 1955

Albert Einstein, the scientist who rewrote science textbooks by discovering $E=mc^2$, the amazing theory of the relationship between space, time, and gravity, was born in Germany on March 14, 1879. His father and his uncle ran an electrical plant. It was there that his interest in science was nurtured as he saw the electrical machines and light.

Albert attended a very strict German school, where he had a hard time adjusting. But something there caught his interest: mathematics and science. Later, when he realized that science was the key to knowing the logic behind the world's creation and the mysteries of the universe, he decided to commit his whole life to scientific research.

Einstein completed his math and physics studies at the Swiss Federal Institute of Technology in four years, and continued studying as he worked at a patent office. He then published a paper called, "On a heuristic point of view concerning the production and transformation of light," and similar papers, causing a revolutionary change in existing theories of light.

After distinguishing himself as a scientist, Einstein published the theory of special relativity, which states that energy of a certain mass equals its mass multiplied by the speed of light squared ($E=mc^2$). He also published the theory of general relativity, which proved that light can bend depending on the force of gravity. As he continued to publish paper after paper, Einstein completely overturned the science field of his day.

Later, Einstein received the highest honor for a scientist, the Nobel Prize, and spent the rest of his years giving lectures and continuing his research. When World War II broke out, he decided to devote the rest of his life to promote world peace. He opposed the use of science to create the atomic bomb and sacrifice innocent lives.

Einstein actively lobbied for peace with activities such as creating a fund to promote peace. Einstein did not cease working until the day of his death in 1955 when he passed away at the age of 76.

알베르트 아인슈타인

물리학자, 1879년 3월 14일~1955년 4월 18일

공간과 시간, 중력에 대한 놀라운 공식 $E=mc^2$를 발표하여 세계 과학 사를 다시 쓴 과학자 아인슈타인은 1879년 3월 14일 독일에서 태어났습니다. 아인슈타인의 아버지는 삼촌과 함께 전기 공장을 운영하셨습니다. 그곳에서 아인슈타인은 전기 기구와 빛을 보며 과학에 대한 호기심을 키워갔습니다.

아인슈타인은 규율이 엄격한 독일의 학교를 다녔습니다. 이런 환경에 적응하지 못한 소년 아인슈타인의 마음을 사로잡은 것은 따로 있었습니다. 바로 수학과 과학이었습니다. 이후 세상 만물의 이치와 우주 세계의 비밀을 풀 수 있는 열쇠가 바로 과학임을 깨달은 그는 평생 연구에 매달리기로 결심합니다.

스위스 취리히의 연방 공과 대학에서 4년간 수학과 물리학 공부에 매진한 아인슈타인은 졸업 후, 특허청의 직원으로 일하면서 연구를 계속합니다. 그리고 〈빛의 발생과 변화에 관련된 발견에 도움이 되는 견해에 대하여〉와 같은 논문을 발표하여 기존의 빛 이론에 혁명적인 변화를 일으켰습니다.

주목 받는 과학자가 된 그는 '어떤 양의 물질이 갖는 에너지는 그 물질의 질량에 빛의 속도의 제곱을 곱한 값과 같다($E=mc^2$)'는 '특수 상대성 이론'과 빛이 중력에 따라 다르게 휘어질 수 있다는 것을 증명한 '일반 상대성 이론'을 계속 내 놓으며 기존의 과학사를 완전히 뒤바꾸었습니다.

이후 아인슈타인은 과학자 최고의 영예인 '노벨 과학상'을 수상하였고, 강연과 연구를 계속하면서 말년을 보냅니다. 그리고 제2차 세계 대전이 발발하자 세계 평화를 위해 남은 생을 헌신하기로 합니다.

그 후, 아인슈타인은 과학을 이용해 원자폭탄을 만들고, 죄 없는 사람들을 희생시키는 것에 반대하였으며, 평화를 위한 기금을 조성하는 등 적극적인 활동을 벌였습니다. 죽는 날까지 자신에게 주어진 일을 멈추지 않았던 그는 1955년, 76세의 나이로 세상을 떠났습니다.

글 · 안형모

어린이들의 꿈을 키워 주는 재미있고 유익한 만화를 만들기 위해 즐겁게 작업하고 있습니다. 인물 이야기를 통해 위인들의 성공적인 업적보다는 성공에 이르기까지 과정과 노력을 담기 위해 노력합니다. 『천추태후』, 『통째로 한국사 1, 2』, 『호동왕자와 낭랑공주』 등의 만화 시나리오를 썼습니다.

그림 · 스튜디오 청비

기발한 상상력을 바탕으로 새롭고 재미있는 콘텐츠를 만들어 내는 만화 창작 집단입니다. 어린이들이 책을 읽고 큰 꿈을 품기를 바라는 마음으로 즐겁게 작업하고 있습니다. 작품으로 『성철 스님』, 『아 다르고 어 다른 우리말 101가지』, 『반기문 유엔 사무총장의 꿈과 도전』 등이 있습니다.

번역 · 자넷 재완 신(Janet Jaywan Shin)

미국 메릴랜드 주에서 태어나고 자랐습니다. 메릴랜드 대학교에서 언어학을 전공하고 UCLA에서 응용언어학 석사 학위를 취득했습니다. 서울대학교 언어교육원에서 전임 강사, 서울대학교 사범대학교 영어교육과에서 초빙교수로 일했습니다. 감수한 책으로 『서울대생한테 비밀 영어과외받기』가 있고 고등학교 영어 교과서 교정 작업에 참여했습니다.

감수 · 김수희

연세대학교에서 역사를 전공했습니다. 이후 한국뿐 아니라 일본, 미국에서 한국어, 일본어, 영어를 가르쳐 왔으며 부모를 위한 영어교육용 책을 썼습니다. 영어교육채널 EBSe '엄마표 영어특강'에서 강의를 하며 홈스쿨, 알파벳과 파닉스, 다차원 테마 영어 수업 기법을 알리고 있습니다. 전국 각지에서 어린이 영어 교육에 대한 강연을 하며 창의적이고 열정적인 교수법으로 영어를 배우고자 하는 어린이와 부모들에게 많은 도움을 주고 있습니다.

Albert Einstein

Albert Einstein enjoyed playing the _____ for the rest of his life.

a. piano
b. cello
c. violin

Answer: c

Contents

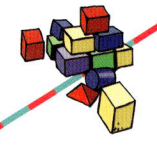

01 .Encounter with a Compass

CD1 Track 01 ▶

Albert Einstein was born on March 14, 1879, in a town called Ulm in the southern part of the German Empire. His parents were concerned that Albert was handicapped because of the unusually large size of his head and the fact that he hadn't started speaking yet.

Two years later, however, around the time his sister Maria was born, Albert began to finally start speaking, so his parents worried less.

You don't think our little Albert has any problems, do you?

I am a little worried, but let's wait and see.

Are you playing with blocks again?

Oh dear!

CRASH

Oh, Albert! Are you okay?

...

The vase fell right next to him and he didn't even flinch! Either he has an amazing ability to concentrate or he's aretarded.

I'm worried about Albert. He's not growing as he should...

Let's wait and see. He just started learning how to talk.

Albert's parents had many concerns because he behaved quite differently from the other children his age. Consequently, they made an effort to observe him carefully and try to meet his unique needs.

Maria, could you tell Albert to come eat lunch?

OK.

16

CD1 Track 05 ▸

First of all, this is how you make a sound, by moving the bow back and forth.
Try it.
SQUEAK
SQUEAK
Wow, that's great, Albert.
Let's practice this over and over again until you get the hang of it.
I don't want to!
Excuse me?

 **Track 07** ▶

Albert sometimes showed signs of autism*. As a result, he would often shock people with his strange behavior.

Albert, are you okay?

Ugh...

Help! Albert looks really sick!

*autism: A mental illness in which one is psychologically out of touch with reality and hides within one's own mind.

Albert's father owned an electrical business. Because Germany at that time was just beginning to disseminate electricity, Einstein's business flourished. As a result, Albert was able to grow up in a wealthy home with few financial difficulties.

We have so many orders to fill that we ran out of some of the components.

Wait a minute. I'll go and buy them.

Mother, what's this?

24

28

29

From that moment on, Albert began to wonder about this invisible force. The compass became an important turning point in Albert's life.

02

The Math-loving Loner

Uncle Jakob, why does the needle of the compass always point north? I can't figure it out.

The magnetic force of the Earth is pulling the magnet in the needle of the compass.

What is magnetic force?

It's the force that's at work between the poles of a magnet. The Earth is like a huge magnet, so there's a magnetic force that exists.

How do we know there's a magnetic force if we can't see it with our eyes?

Geez! You sure have a lot of questions. No one can deny that you're the son of an engineer.

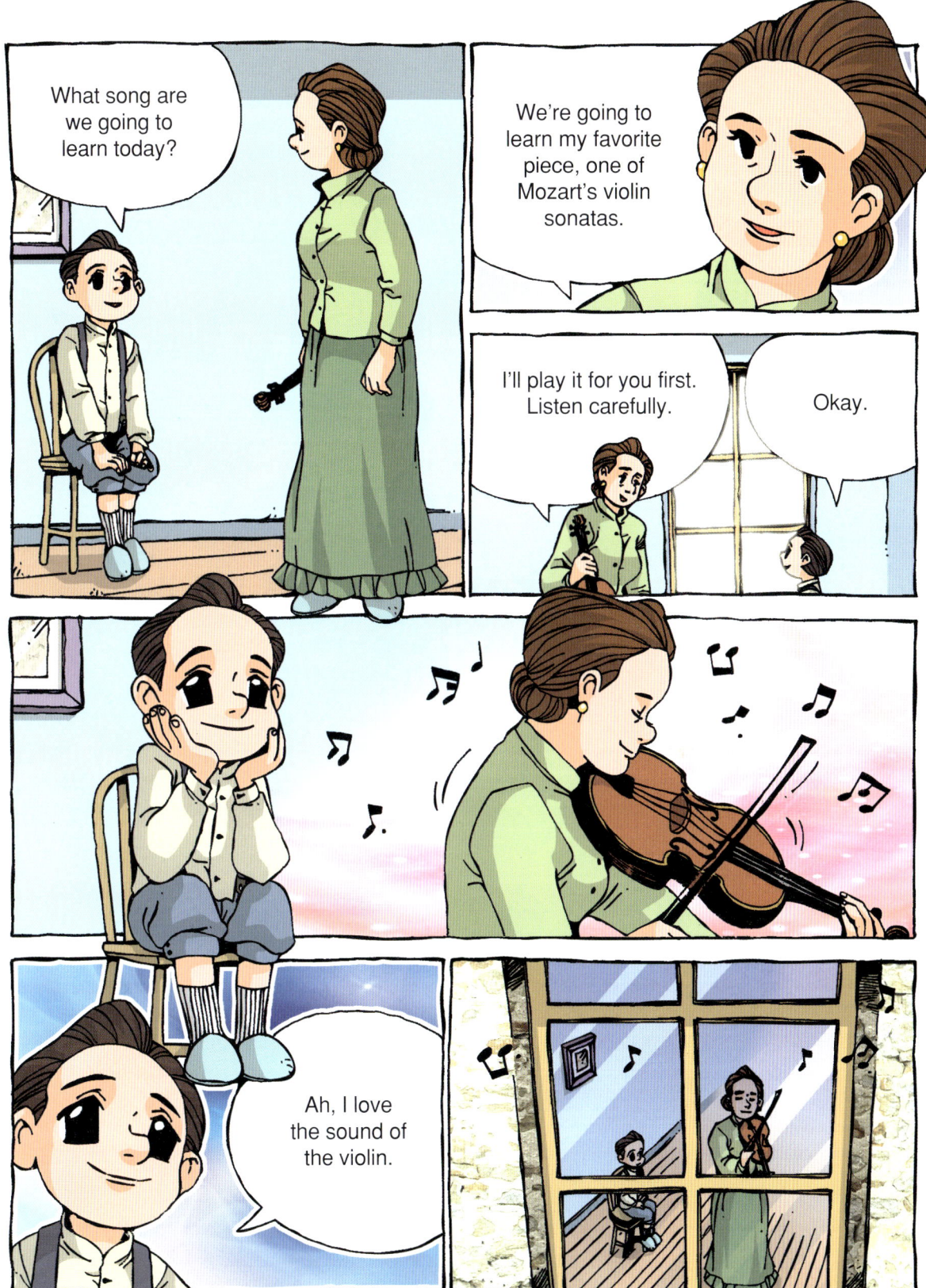

 Track 14 ▶

It soon came time for Albert to enter elementary school. Jewish children usually attended Jewish schools, but Albert attended a Catholic school.

Just because you're Jewish doesn't mean you need to attend a Jewish school. Going to a Catholic school will be better for your future here in Germany.

Do whatever the teacher tells you to do, and make a lot of friends at school.

Yes, Mother.

Bye-bye.

His personality has gotten a lot more easy-going, but I'm still worried about him. They say that German schools are pretty strict. I wonder how well he'll adjust...

Albert's parents' concerns were not unfounded. Albert had a difficult time adjusting at school.

Albert, it might not matter to you very much that you're Jewish. But it could bother the other students very much.

Why?

The Jews committed a crime against humanity that cannot be forgiven.

Look at this!

Jesus Christ died with nails this big, driven into his hands and feet. It's because of you Jews!

The Jews made Jesus die?

42

I heard that Greek has letters that represent vowels. How are they used?

Why are you wondering this all of a sudden?

I think it's important to learn the principles of a language before learning its alphabet.

I'm not going to answer any questions that aren't related to today's lesson. All you need to do is memorize what I teach you.

Yes, sir.

Yes, sir.

Have you all memorized the words I gave you for homework?

Let's have each student recite three words, starting with those sitting in the front.

araba, aslan, afendis.*

*araba: car / aslan: lion, tiger / afendis: teacher

*meydan: town square / at: horse / pita: bread

Zero percent?

You get low scores like this because you hate memorizing? You impudent boy!

Albert's free-spirited personality did not mix well with the strict, authoritarian environment of German schools of that time period.

Your mentality is completely wrong!

...

Albert couldn't get used to school life and felt more and more out of place.

What a terrible day today.

Albert encountered mathematics for the first time through the suggestion of his uncle, who had studied engineering. After looking at a mathematics book, Albert quickly fell in love with the subject.

*Euclid's Elements: A study arranged by a Greek philosopher named Euclid, dealing with the mathematical characteristics of space and the measurement of the lengths, widths, and angles of shapes.

03 Longing for Freedom for the Soul

In 1889, Albert completed elementary school and entered Luitpold Gymnasium*.

Congratulations.

Congratulations, Albert.

Well, all German schools are a bit like that.

Congratulations? Is a prep school going to be any different? They're just going to teach us to cover our papers and memorize, too.

I wish an older student would mentor Albert in his studies.

At that time, Germany was under the influence of Prime Minister Otto von Bismarck, who had a military background. As a result, there was a military influence on many aspects of society.

*Gymnasium: A preparatory school in Germany.

In schools, for example, classes were conducted in a military fashion, to the point where teachers were called general.

I apologize for my tardiness, General!

Tardiness warrants a punishment. Stand over there.

Albert hated this kind of military-style education.

Nothing's different.

I've told you this over and over again, but language is learned through repetition.

You need to memorize whatever words or grammar rules I tell you. Do you understand?

Yes, sir!

Learning by rote memory is so dreadful.

Germany,
Germany above all~ 🎵

Whoa, they look like mindless robots!

We're taught to unconditionally follow and memorize things so that we'll become mindless robots, too.

Albert! You don't want to cheer for our army? Why aren't you clapping for them?

It looks like you need some more moral training. Come out to the school yard.

I don't know the anthem.

If you don't know it, you can at least try to pretend!

62

Then one day, Albert met Max Talmud, a medical student. He joined the Einsteins once a week for dinner, in accordance with Jewish custom.

This student is going to eat dinner with us every Thursday.

My name is Max Talmud. Nice to meet you.

Nice to meet you, too.

Oh, those are Albert's books. He's attending a gymnasium prep school.

You must have a college student living here.

A gymnasium student can solve these difficult problems?

Is there something wrong with my books?

Oh!

64

Wait and see! Science is going to change the world someday.

I like science a lot, too.

Oh yeah? I have the complete scientific series called the *Bernstein Series*. Do you want to read it?

Yes, please!

Albert had always been interested in science, but he became even more interested after meeting Max Talmud.

The more you know about science, the more amazing it is.

Who knows? There might be a huge world out there in space, created by beings far more superior to humans.

66

Albert, who was now in his teenage years, was growing up and experiencing many changes.

One of the major changes was in his home. His father's business failed, which brought on financial hardship.

Let's close the factory and move to Italy.

We can't rely on the electrical industry of Germany anymore, but things are just beginning in Italy.

Our business could do really well there.

Let's do that. I'm getting tired of living in Munich.

But...

Albert's family moved to Italy, while Albert remained in Germany.

Albert's life by himself in Germany seemed to drag on day after day.

Left, move forward!

You idiot! Can't you follow the orders?

71

At that time, many different territories were united within the German Empire. In order to maintain order in society, Prime Minister Bismarck stressed the independence and unity of people groups. He also increased military power to keep public order.

As the military became stronger, elements of military culture such as commands, obedience, and punishment, infiltrated society. Schools were no exception.

Even if the grammar is wrong, you can figure out the meaning if you know the meaning of the words.

That's why I tell you to just memorize as many words as possible.

Did everyone copy the vocabulary words twenty times like I said?

Yes!

74

Alright. As you wish. Come out to the front!

Don't study anymore if you hate it that much!

We don't need students like you at school. No one would have a problem if you left our school.

How can you say that?

Why not? I have every right to say that when the classroom environment gets polluted by worthless students like you!

Albert couldn't deal with the strict, systematic education system of Germany. In the end, he ended up leaving Luitpold Gymnasium at the age of fifteen.

There are some schools that admit students without a high school diploma. This should help.

Thank you.

In December, 1894, Albert left Germany to join his family in Italy.

04

Light—
The Coming
of a Physicist

CD1 Track 36 ▶

Albert?

Albert!

What are you doing here? What about school?

I'm sorry, Mother. I... withdrew from school.

You did?

What?

I tried to hang on, but it was just too hard.

Maria, go get your father.

So you're saying that you dropped out of school?

I'm sorry, Father.

This is not something to be sorry about! What kind of job are you going to get without a high school diploma?

I heard there's a school in Switzerland, the Swiss Federal Institute of Technology Zurich, which doesn't require a high school diploma to take the entrance exam.

It makes me sad to see Mother and Father looking so depressed because of me.

People like me should never have been born.

83

I'll teach you everything there is to know at the plant. Hahaha!

We believe in you, Albert. Find what you really want to do and go for it.

Thank you, Father.

While Albert was preparing to enter university, he was also traveling and helping his father at the plant whenever time allowed.

Around this time, Albert became interested in the very thing that would mold his future destiny—light.

Where does this connect to?

I'll connect it. Why don't you put it over there next to the generator?

84

Huh?

What did you do to make the electricity go out?

I don't know. I think I moved one of the lines by mistake...

Move over!

Wow! It became bright in an instant. That's so neat.

That Albert, he's totally absorbed in a book again.

Wow! I never knew physics was such a fascinating field.

When I enter university, I want to study more about physics.

Father, I think I want to take the entrance exam at the Swiss Federal Institute of Technology Zurich.

Aren't you still underage?

I have a certificate from my gymnasium math teacher.

He said that that would help. It might help qualify me to take the entrance exam.

If you're serious about it, then give it a try.

Okay, I will.

Thanks to the letter that Albert's math teacher had written him, he barely met the requirements to take the Swiss Federal Institute of Technology Zurich exam.

Good luck on the exam!

Don't worry. I'll pass with flying colors.

Go Albert!

Unfortunately, although Albert took the exam with confidence, he received horrible results.

His scores in math and physics were outstanding, but he did poorly in subjects that require memorization such as French and history. As a result, he failed the exam.

Is this far as I can go?

I can't believe I failed!

Good luck on the exam!

Go Albert!

My family will be so disappointed when they find out.

Are you Albert Einstein?

Yes, how did you know?

90

I'm the dean of the Institute. You didn't pass the exam because you didn't do well in the humanities section, but you did very well in the mathematics and science sections.

Why don't you spend a year completing the high school curriculum? Then I'll make sure you can enter our school next year.

Wow, really?

Thank you so much for your consideration.

Haha. Of course.

Alright! I'm going to make a new start.

Albert followed the dean's advice and studied for one year at Aarau Canton School. This school's relaxed environment was different from Germany's gymnasiums. Albert was able to exercise his creativity as much as he wanted to there.

91

In the liberal environment of Aarau Canton School, Albert was able to concentrate on science and spend more and more time studying. It was also then that Albert decided that he wanted to become a physicist.

05 Pursuing His Dream and Love amidst Poverty

Now I can really get into studying physics. This is where I'll fulfill my dream of becoming a theoretical physicist.

The following year, Einstein graduated from Aarau Canton School and entered the Swiss Federal Institute of Technology Zurich.

There were many world renowned professors at the Swiss Federal Institute of Technology Zurich.

Read this book by Professor Weber. It's really good.

One of the professors who took an interest in Einstein ever since he took the entrance exam was a famous physicist named Heinrich Weber.

Professor Weber is Europe's top physicist, so this book must be good. Thanks.

Professsor Weber...

*Maxwell: A Scottish physicist.
*Newton's law of motion: The relationship between the force that acts on an object and the movement of the object, formally discovered by Newton.

Professor, the student who asked a question in class today is Albert Einstein. He's the one who scored well last year on the science section of the entrance exam but didn't pass the exam.

Ah, I remember. The one whom I gave permission to sit in on my class.

This year, he must've passed the exam. I'd better go and congratulate him.

Professor Weber's theories are too outdated.

I want to study cutting-edge physics like electromagnetism. It's so frustrating to have to study theories that are obsolete.

My theories are outdated?

Pr-
Professor!

Forget about congratulating him. Let's go!

Wasn't that Professor Weber?

Albert, I think he heard you. Oh no!

. . .

Speed is relative.

Depending on the direction of the movement, the same speed could be faster or slower.

When Einstein was curious about something, he would ask right away. However his professors considered his stance as a challenge to their authority, and usually ignored his questions.

Then does that mean that the speed of light could also change?

The speed of light is always constant.

That's strange. If the speed of everything else changes, but the speed of light doesn't change, isn't that a violation of a law of nature?

He's trying to challenge every single thing I say.

Weber, who was especially conservative, viewed Einstein's behavior negatively.

Several scientists have tried to prove it, but failed. If you're so confident, you can research it yourself.

Let's end today's class here.

He thinks inquisitiveness about academic studies is defiance of authority. Then does he expect us to just memorize the things that have already been proven?

The stiff environment here is just like the gymnasium's.

Albert, even if there's something that you don't agree with, just let it go.

You know that Professor Weber only acknowledges things that have been proven through experiments. Just accept it.

Accept it? I have to prove it through experiments, too.

What? What kind of experiment can you do?

This experiment is dangerous, so you need to follow the directions precisely. Everyone understand?

I want to prove the true nature of light.

Don't! He said we have to follow his instructions precisely.

You just watch.

Oh, the professor's coming!

A-Albert!

Gasp!

FZZZ

KABcoM

Aaaaah!

Grrrrr!

Who is responsible for this havoc? Confess at once!

Why did you not follow my instructions and just do as you pleased? Do you take me for a fool?

From now on, Einstein is not to be allowed in the laboratory outside of class time.

Yes, sir.

Hello, Professor.

Hmph!

106

The professors treated Einstein coldly. Faced with their indifference, Einstein lost interest in his classes and began to spend more and more time by himself.

I miss the days at Aarau High School.

Albert...

*vehicle: A material that establishes an interaction between two matters.

Then what is ether? Are you saying it's a material that doesn't exist?

That's right. There's a high chance that it's just a figment of the imagination.

Professor Weber would be furious if he heard that.

That's just too bad. The academic world improves and develops only as wrong notions get corrected. We have to be able to say if something is wrong.

Albert's not wrong, but it's this attitude that the professors don't like about him. It worries me.

The graduation exam is coming up, and you're not even coming to class. What are you going to do?

I've already given up on my studies.

What are you talking about? These are the notes from class you need to know. Study them.

Thanks, Marcel.

I guess you do care somewhat about your studies.

What are you going to do after graduation?

I want to stay here and continue doing research.

If you're thinking of staying, you'd better work on raising your grades.

Around the time of graduation, Einstein, who wanted to stay and continue his studies, was suddenly faced with a crisis.

His father's company went bankrupt so his family suddenly had no money.

Albert, I feel terrible to give you this unhappy news.

The company went bankrupt and I can no longer send you money for your tuition and living allowance. You're going to have to earn your own tuition and spending money.

Bankrupt?

He's put his whole life into that business. He must be devastated.

Father...

I can't be another burden on him. I've got to earn my own living now.

With his family's financial situation in mind, Einstein looked into working as a teaching assistant after graduating from university.

However, despite the fact that he graduated with excellent grades, none of the professors hired him or even wrote him a letter of recommendation.

No worries. I'm thinking of sending my resume to every university in Europe. They can't all reject me, right?

Albert, you already sent a letter to every university in Europe.

What?

But I have yet to receive a single reply letter.

How-how could this be?

Albert...

In addition to not having any financial means due to his father's bankruptcy, Einstein couldn't find a job, leaving him in a difficult situation.

1905, the Year of Miracles

After graduation, Einstein and Maric continued their relationship. However, because of their financial difficulties, they spent many of their days unhappily.

Mileva, don't we have any snacks? I'm so hungry.

You know we don't. We barely have enough to get by with the money that my parents send us.

Why don't you go out and try to find a job?

I desperately want to, but there aren't any decent job openings.

I don't know how we're going to make it.

I'm going to go and stay in Hungary for a while.

I should have found a secure job by now. Mileva, I feel so ashamed.

Mileva was tired of their life of poverty and had also failed the teacher's exam. She had to forfeit her dream of becoming a teacher and return to her homeland.

After Mileva left, Einstein's life became even more destitute.

I'm so hungry that I can't even concentrate on my book.

Sigh. Is there any hope in my life?

One day, in the midst of his difficult days, Einstein received an unexpected letter. It was from his college friend, Marcel Grossman.

Huh?
There's a letter in the mailbox.

Albert, I found a job opening for you. Hurry and come to Bern!

Job opening?

This is the head of the Swiss patent office, Fredrich Huller.

Hello.

I heard about your situation.

With the help of his friend Marcel, Einstein was hired as a second class technical examiner at the Swiss Federal Patent Bureau.

Once he started his new job, Einstein's life began to improve. Einstein wanted his parents, who had always worried about him, to be the first to see that he was doing well now.

Unfortunately, he wasn't able to. His father had suddenly passed away. His father was the one who had introduced him to the existence of an invisible force through a compass.

Einstein didn't wallow in his sadness however. In order to establish the stable life that his father had wished for him, he started a family with Mileva Maric.

And he began his research on light and gravity that he had been meaning to do for a long time.

Can I help you?

I'm here to... register my patent.

123

But I can't believe the claim yet because I've never seen it for myself.

But what if I think of myself as light?

If I were walking inside of a train before it took off, my walking speed would be the same as that of a person walking outside on the street.

But if the train were going 100 kilometers per hour, and I were walking inside, in the same direction as the train, what speed would I be going? I would look like I was walking at a normal pace to the people inside the train, but not to the people outside the train. I would look like I was moving at an incredible speed, the speed of the train plus the speed I was walking.

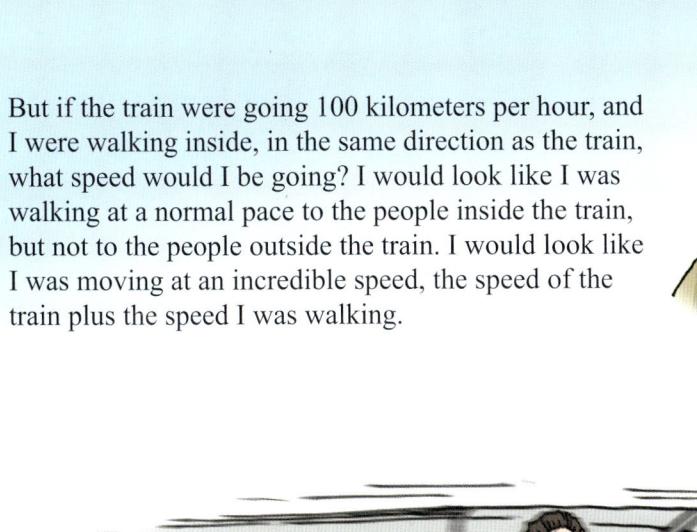

That's incredible!

You understand? I've finished my explanation now.

Yes! The speed of light is always constant.

But because time flows differently depending on the situation in which people encounter it, the speed will seem different!

The faster the speed—in other words, the faster a speed approaches the speed of light—the slower time flows.

What are you talking about? Then time doesn't flow at the same speed for everyone?

Right. Time is moving slower for the person who is in motion than for the person who is standing still.

There is no absolute time nor absolute space in this world. All motion is relative.

Oh, that is an astounding theory! Let's patent that immediately!

Patent?

I'm sorry, honey.

After much research on light and speed, Einstein established the theory of relativity, the theory that there is no such thing as absolute time or space, but rather that time and space are both relative.

And in 1905, Einstein was able to finally put together and publish four important research papers, including one on his research on the theory of relativity involving light and speed.

There's another Einstein who authored a paper about a bold idea and got it published in a scientific journal, but the Einstein here doesn't do much.

Look at this, Einstein.

I know, right?

Should I try to publish a plausible paper, too?

Stop dreaming! If you publish a paper in a scientific journal, then I'm going to win the Nobel Prize.

Congratulations, Einstein! Your paper that was published is getting a good response.

Thank you.

This Einstein is you?

Bring it over here please.

What is all this?

It's your shelf and other furniture to put in your study.

THUMP

*E=mc² : E=energy, m=mass, c=speed of light

This is it, exactly! Hahaha!

Three months after Einstein published the theory of relativity, he published the groundbreaking theory of $E=mc^2$.

This theory of the value of mass and energy having an equivalence implies that when the nucleus of an atom divides into lighter nuclei, the mass reduces slightly but creates a massive amount of energy.

This theory, which astonished the world, later tragically led to the creation of the atomic bomb, for which Einstein deeply regretted it.

133

07 The Lonely Genius

CD2 Track 20 ▶

Even after Einstein published four groundbreaking papers, life continued as normal for Albert Einstein.

This can't be. How strange.

The reason was scientists at that time did not realize just how great these findings were.

What's wrong?

There's no response whatsoever. Is it because I wrote these papers in my spare time, and didn't put enough effort into them?

Why don't you wait a little longer? Something good is bound to happen.

Just as Einstein's wife had predicted, not much time passed before the theory of special relativity was acknowledged among scientists. Then the opportunity for Einstein to become the physicist he always wanted to be finally arrived.

Albert, you got a letter from a professor at the Swiss Federal Institute of Technology Zurich.

I wonder what it's about.

Dear Mr. Einstein,

We would like to offer you a position here as a professor.

Pr-professor?

When Alfred Kleiner, a physics professor at the Swiss Federal Institute of Technology Zurich, read Einstein's paper, he predicted that Einstein would become a famous physicist.

I'm going to miss the patent office.

In 1909, Einstein left the patent office and began teaching students at his alma mater.

Einstein gained popularity among students wearing casual clothes at the podium and teaching with passion.

I'll bet you Professor Einstein's going to be wearing short pants again today.

And I'll bet you he's going to be holding a note in his hand.

Hello!

I told you he'd be wearing short pants!

I was right, too.

Heh heh heh

Let's get started for today!

Yes, sir!

Alright, say there are five matches. If the length of one match is 2.5 inches, then how long would five matches be?

12.5 inches.

I knew that's what you would say. But I seriously doubt that answer.

Why?

I don't believe in exact mathematical calculations.

Or maybe you are not good at mathematics?

The University of Berlin has the best science departments in the world. Every scientist would love to work there. I will seriously consider your offer.

The theory of special relativity is not complete, but many scholars are showing so much interest in it.

I need to hurry and strengthen the theory.

Unlike Einstein's success and recognition as a scholar, his family life was not going well. As time passed, his relationship with his wife became more and more distant.

Gag!

Am I... pregnant?

I'm home.

Dear, you know, I...

Let's talk later. I just thought of something to strengthen the special relativity theory.

Sigh!

Einstein's personality was such that once he became absorbed in his research, he couldn't pay attention to anything else.

He would sometimes even have discussions with students while standing in the rain or snow, and be unfazed as he recorded calculations in his notebook.

Against Mileva's wishes, Einstein took the position at the University of Berlin.

But Mileva did not adjust well to life in Germany.

They said our second son is mentally handicapped.

What?

We need to move somewhere else. Let's go somewhere with a better environment, for the sake of our son's health.

How could this happen?

You're really going to go to Switzerland without me?

We need to, for the baby's sake.

That year in August, World War I erupted. Austria and Germany formed an alliance and fought against England, France, and the USSR.

Those people who do research for a living, don't they think about the masses of young people who are dying in the war?

By all means possible, the expansion of this war must be thwarted.

At the outbreak of the world war, 93 scholars made a public statement showing support for Germany's aggressive takeovers.

We agree that Germany is not responsible for acts of brutality and we recognize that military action is necessary.

How can people really believe that?

No! The voice of those who oppose the war must also be heard, right now.

Everyone, this war needs to come to an end! Europe needs to be united as one and live in peace!

That's not true! The day is quickly coming when England's battleships will sink and London will be burned to the ground. Let's support the German military.

WOOOOOO!

Is it really true that there is no way to stop this war?

Einstein was in anguish because there was nothing he could do to stop the war.

He withdrew to a quiet house in the outskirts of Berlin and turned his attention, instead, to fixing weak points of the special relativity theory.

145

Einstein spent much time alone, away from his family, working on his research.

Only his cousin Elsa Lowenthal came by once in a while to take care of him.

Then three years later, in 1916, Einstein completed the revision of the special relativity theory, and created the general theory of relativity.

It's finally finished.

Congratulations, Albert!

You did it! How did you even think of the idea that space is warped?

I wanted to make the theory applicable to any situation, not just to special cases, as the special relativity theory did.

Einstein's general theory of relativity was an intriguing theory which revealed an unknown aspect about the universe.

After Einstein published his latest theory, several scientists set out to test his theory.

The universe is warped by the gravitational force of matter? That is a fascinating theory, indeed.

According to the theory, all matter that is in motion moves in the same shape as warped space. The same is true for light.

I want to see if this theory is really true.

In 1919, Arthur Eddington, a British astronomer, proved that Einstein's theory was correct with photographs that he had taken of a solar eclipse.

Consequently, Einstein was able to join the ranks of the world's top scientists.

How did the photographs of the eclipse turn out?

It's true! The light is bent, just as Dr. Einstein's theory predicts.

The theory of relativity impacted not only scientists, but philosophers, artists, and everyone interested in the universe and nature.

Yay! It's Dr. Einstein!

You're amazing, Dr. Einstein!

08 A Lifelong Pacifist

 **Track 27** ▶

After the theory of relativity was proven, Einstein's status as a scientist was altered completely.

The newspaper talks of nothing else but the theory of relativity.

Not only the newspapers, but there's even a cigarette that's named after him.

Anyway, Einstein's an incredible man.

Hmph! How much can a Jewish man do?

Dr. Einstein?

*Zionist Movement: A movement among Jewish people scattered around the world to reestablish their national homeland.

Hitler is all over the newspapers.

Albert, don't be alarmed, but I just got word that your mother has passed away.

Wh-what?

Around that time, Einstein's mother, Pauline, who had loved him very much, passed away due to cancer.

Mother...

It saddened Einstein even more to think about how hard her life was as a Jew.

I have been living the life of a Jew all along.

Einstein felt pity for the life of persecution that Jews lived, and began to slowly participate in the Zionist Movement.

I am a human, a good European citizen, and I have always been thankful that I am Jewish.

You are finally making a stand, Dr. Einstein!

I am very happy to be able to represent the Jewish people as I stand here today.

YAYYYY!

He doesn't think as German citizens do. We can't let him continue like this.

At that time, Germany was trying to avoid criticism of their defeat in World War I and their current economic depression by finding something to turn people's attention away.

So they turned their focus on the Jews. The first person they targeted was Albert Einstein, who was not only a Jew but also an anti-war activist.

As Einstein began participating in the Zionist Movement, criticism began to emerge from many directions.

Dr. Einstein, please don't take part in the Zionist Movement anymore. Something is strange in the way Germans are beginning to treat Jews.

The Secretary of Finance has been assassinated, and the Secretary of Foreign Affairs, who was a Jew, has also been assassinated. You may also be in serious danger.

I am just speaking as one citizen who embraces peace.

This is unrelated to politics. I'm just acting on my personal beliefs, seeking peace and freedom.

But Einstein's efforts could not be realized. As the Nazis began to have more influence in Germany, people began to believe blindly that Germany was superior to all. This sentiment began to dominate the country.

The greatest people in the world are pure Germans. The Jews and Communists need to be done away with!

Yayyy!

The Jews are taking away our jobs. Let's kick them out of our country!

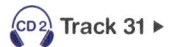

Even as he was receiving death threats, Einstein was also receiving invitations from all over the world to speak. He decided to leave Germany and travel the world to give lectures.

One day as he was returning from a speaking engagement in Japan, he received notice that he had been awarded the Nobel Prize for Physics.

Dr. Einstein!

You've been selected to receive the Nobel Prize for Physics!

That is wonderful.

Congratulations!

Thank you.

After being awarded the Nobel Prize and gaining more fame, Einstein returned to Berlin in 1924. He began to concentrate on opposing war and advocating peace by giving lectures and writing editorials on his opinions.

In whatever circumstances, we have to make an effort to create peace!

Yayyyy!

158

Hitler has taken over Germany completely. He's expanding his military power and persecuting the Jews ruthlessly.

Oh no!

I heard they even have a price on your head. If you stay in Germany, Hitler will most certainly kill you.

This day has finally come upon us.

The oppression of the Jews grew out of control, and Einstein had no choice but to leave Germany.

This is the way I have to leave Germany...

Einstein emigrated to America and worked at the Institute for Advanced Study in Princeton, keeping a low profile.

In 1939, Germany's chancellor, Adolf Hitler, declared that the land where Germans were living all belonged to Germany, and began invading neighboring countries.

This is absurd!

This was the beginning of the second World War, which would bring upon suffering to all the nations of the world.

The Second World War? Hitler is the one who is behind this huge catastrophe.

Around the start of World War II, Einstein received a letter.

Dear Dr. Einstein,

My name is Lise Meitner. I am a Jewish chemist who had studied radioactive elements in Germany.

160

I escaped Germany when the persecution of the Jews became too fierce. The scientists with whom I worked on nuclear fission are still there in Germany. Germans are trying to use their knowledge to create an atomic bomb. If they succeed in making a bomb, the results will be devastating.

Atomic bomb?

H-how? Nuclear fission stemmed from the theory of $E=mc^2$ and fission is being used to produce atomic bombs!

Being the peace activist that he was, Einstein could not bear the fact that his theory was being utilized to make a nuclear bomb.

I did not develop this theory so they could make bombs with it. How could this happen?

Einstein could not bear to think about the terrible truth that Germany, the country which started the war, was armed with a nuclear bomb.

I've got to stop this if it's the last thing I do.

If Germany creates an atomic bomb, thousands of people will lose their lives.

Dr. Einstein, why don't you write to the President of the United States and advise him to make an atomic bomb before the Germans do?

What?

Einstein agonized for several sleepless nights over whether to write a letter or not.

If America makes an atomic bomb, it will still be a weapon that will take many lives. The end result will be the same.

After Einstein struggled with this issue, he signed a letter to President Franklin D. Roosevelt about the necessity of developing an atomic bomb.

But stopping Hitler from developing a bomb is more urgent.

After receiving Einstein's letter, the U.S. immediately began to develop a nuclear bomb.

In August, 1945, the atomic bomb, which originated in this way, was dropped on Hiroshima and then Nagasaki, two cities in Japan.

Japan, stunned by the devastating force of the bombs, surrendered immediately. Hundreds of thousands of people either died or were injured.

Afterwards, Einstein began to actively protest the development of nuclear arms. He headed the Emergency Committee of Atomic Scientists, which was created to regulate nuclear arms development.

Nuclear arms development is the responsibility of scientists.

We have now clearly seen the power that science possesses.

As members of society, we have to take proper responsibility for how the results of our research will affect society.

World War II ended and peace was restored once again, but Einstein faced another kind of war.

Jews have lived a difficult life for too long, as wanderers without their own land.

An intense conflict over territory, between the Jews and the Arabs, had erupted.

Einstein began to support the establishment of Israel's nationhood after finding out that 600,000 Jews were being threatened by the Arab military.

And at last, on May 14, 1948, Israel declared independence, marking the birth of the nation of Israel.

Finally, the nation of the Jews has been established. How delighted Mother and Father would be if they knew about this.

Dr. Einstein, I'm here to relay a message to you from the Prime Minister of Israel.

From the Prime Minister?

What does it concern?

Currently, the position of president of Israel is vacant.

167

I would also like to do more for Israel, but I have lived my whole life as a physicist.

I will quietly cheer for the newly built nation of Israel from where I am.

I understand. I will pass on your words to the citizens of Israel.

Being asked to be the president was quite an honor, but Einstein did not believe that that was the right path for him.

He was quite content with having been able to research as much as he wanted, live the life of a physicist, and get a little closer to discovering the secrets of the universe.

He was spending his days peacefully, when suddenly Einstein's health deteriorated rapidly due to a blood vessel rupture.

Ahh!

Dr. Einstein!

Even on his death bed, Einstein was doing research on the unified field theory*. On April 16, 1955, Einstein breathed his last breath, and quietly passed away at the age of 76.

After living a life of courage, Einstein's death was humble and quiet just like his life.

Einstein spent his life researching about light and publishing many papers. He completely changed mankind's understanding of time, space, and the universe.

The world has lost its best scientist, and we have lost our best friend.

The theories that he had left behind are still being applied to our daily lives even today.

His theories have led to the invention of the automatic door, digital camera, video camera, copy machine, solar battery, breathanalyzer, and street lamps that are regulated by light.

*unified field theory: A theory which attempts to explain all forms and relationships of forces that operate between particles with one concept.

The new findings about the world Einstein discovered in his lifetime were not just relevant to the realm of science. They were discoveries so great that they affected the lives of all of mankind.

During the course of my life, I have simply been trying to see nature's laws at work, even just for a moment.

If you look at the universe closely, you, too, will see its beautiful harmony.

Einstein's funeral was conducted in a simple manner. In accordance with his request not to have a grave made, his ashes were sprinkled over a river.

Father.

That you may have eternal rest...

Einstein spent his life looking for the secrets of the universe. While seeking truth, loving peace, and possessing the pure passion of a scientist, he published countless papers for the benefit of mankind. He never betrayed his conscience as a scientist and acted as a peace activist, as well.

With his life, Einstein made us realize how much can be accomplished with a love for nature and people, and showed us how to live as responsible people. The great accomplishments of this genius physicist and true peace activist will be an eternal light for mankind now and far into the future.

Word Search

● Find the words which are hidden horizontally, vertically and diagonally.

```
Q M Z G Q M Z G Q M Z G Q M Z G Q M Z G Q M T
W S T G U G G L E N A H W W N A H W N O
E B Q J A B Q J E T B A R B A R I C B M
R V C K R V C K R V C K R R V C K R V M
E C D L T C V L T C D L T T C D U T C E
V X E Q Y X E O Y X E Q Y Y X E N Y X M
E Z V W U D V W C Z V W U U Z V J U Z W
A A A E I A E E I A R E I I A R A I A I
L S S R O S G C O S T R O O S G S O S T
P D C T P D H T O D H E P P D H T P D H
A F A Y A F U Y A T U Y A A F U Y A F D
S G S U S G I N T R I G U I N G U S G R
D H S I D H O I D H O I D D H O I D H A
F J A B S O R B F J T J F F J T J F J W
G K N B G K R E C E P I E N T S B G K C
H L A N H L E N H L E N H H L E N H L E
J Q T M J Q T A U T H O R I T Y M J Q T
L W E Q L W Q L W Y Q L L W Y Q L W Y
Z W K F Z W K F Z W K F Z Z S U F T E R
X E M E X A M I N E R U X X E M U X E M
C R Q C C R Q C P C I G H T R Q C C R Q
```

intriguing	reveal	advocate	barbaric
withdraw	absorb	authority	examiner

Lesson 2

Vocabulary

● Match each word to the correct meaning.

1. pacifist   • 유대인

2. encounter   • 공석의

3. establishment   • 평화주의자

4. Jew   • 마주치다

5. vacant   • 설립

6. deteriorate   • 영역

7. realm   • 악화하다

8. accomplishment   • 적용할 수 있는

9. revision   • 휘다

10. relativity   • 상대성

11. warp   • 개정

12. applicable   • 업적

Guess What?

- Guess what he said in the blank.

Wait and see! Science is going to change the world someday.

I like science a lot, too.

Yes, please!

Oh yeah? I have the complete scientific series called the *Bernstein Series*. Do you want to read it?

Albert had always been interested in science, but he became even more interested after meeting Max Talmud.

Who knows? There might be a huge world out there in space, created by beings far more superior to humans.

Lesson 4

Time Controller

What would it be like if you could control time?

1. If you could control time, would you want to speed it up, or slow it down? And why?

_____

_____

2. Would you want to go into the future or into the past? And how would the period be different from today?

_____

_____

3. Draw the picture of your time travel.

How Big How Small

There are some physics words for measuring how huge or how tiny things are. We use the words such as 'Giga' 'Mega' 'Kilo' 'Nano'... not only in physics but also in everyday life. Let's learn the special but basic physics words here.

PREFIXES	VALUE	STANDARD FORM	SYMBOL
Tera	1000 000 000 000	10^{12}	T
Giga	1000 000 000	10^{9}	G
Mega	1000 000	10^{6}	M
Kilo	1000	10^{3}	k
deci	0.1	10^{-1}	d
centi	0.01	10^{-2}	c
milli	0.001	10^{-3}	m
micro	0.000 001	10^{-6}	μ
nano	0.000 000 001	10^{-9}	n
pico	0.000 000 000 001	10^{-12}	p

Physics Information

There are relationships which are invisible everywhere around us. Physicists understood how they work and keep the regular relations, then made formulae explaining the relationships. These are some of the basic physics formulae for some relationships.

▲ The relationship between average speed, distance, and time.

$$\text{average speed (평균 속도)} = \frac{\text{distance (거리)}}{\text{time (시간)}}$$

▲ The relationship between force, mass, and acceleration.

$$\text{force (힘)} = \text{mass (질량)} \times \text{acceleration (가속도)}$$

$$\text{acceleration (가속도)} = \frac{\text{change in velocity (속도의 변화)}}{\text{time taken (걸린 시간)}}$$

▲ The relationship between density, mass, volume.

$$\text{density (밀도)} = \frac{\text{mass (질량)}}{\text{volume (부피)}}$$

1879년   3월 14일, 독일 울름에서 태어납니다.

1881년   2세   가족이 모두 함께 뮌헨으로 이사갑니다.

1888년   9세   초등학교에 입학합니다.

1894년   15세   고등학교를 중퇴하고 이탈리아에 있는 가족에게 갑니다.

1895년   16세   고등학교를 졸업하기 위해 스위스의 학교에 입학합니다.

1897년   18세   취리히 공과대학에서 물리학을 공부하기 시작합니다.

1902년   23세   베른에 있는 스위스 특허청에서 일하기 시작합니다.
                아버지가 돌아가십니다.

1903년   24세   대학 동기였던 밀레바 마리치와 결혼합니다.

1904년   25세   맏아들 한스 알베르트가 태어납니다.

1905년   26세   특수 상대성 이론을 설명한 과학 논문 네 편이 발표됩니다.

1912년   33세   취리히 공과대학의 물리학과 교수가 됩니다.

1914년   35세   제1차 세계대전이 발발합니다.

1916년   37세   특수 상대성 이론을 보강한 일반 상대성 이론을 발표합니다.

1918년	39세	제1차 세계대전이 끝납니다.
1919년	40세	개기 일식으로 일반 상대성 이론이 증명되었습니다.
1920년	41세	어머니가 돌아가십니다.
1921년	42세	노벨 물리학상을 받습니다. 미국으로 시온주의를 지지하기 위한 강연 여행을 떠납니다.
1926년	47세	통일장 이론을 연구합니다.
1933년	54세	히틀러의 나치스가 독일에서 권력을 잡습니다.
1939년	60세	제2차 세계대전이 발발합니다. 미국 대통령에게 독일이 원자 폭탄을 제조하고 있음을 알립니다.
1940년	61세	미국 시민이 됩니다.
1945년	66세	최초의 원자 폭탄 '리틀보이'가 일본 히로시마에 떨어집니다. 제2차 세계대전이 끝납니다.
1952년	73세	이스라엘로부터 대통령이 되어달라는 요청을 받지만 거절합니다.
1955년	76세	4월 18일, 사망합니다.

Note

who? 01	Barack Obama	978-89-6370-514-9
who? 02	Charles Darwin	978-89-6370-515-6
who? 03	Bill Gates	978-89-6370-516-3
who? 04	Hillary Clinton	978-89-6370-517-0
who? 05	Stephen Hawking	978-89-6370-518-7
who? 06	Oprah Winfrey	978-89-6370-519-4
who? 07	Steven Spielberg	978-89-6370-520-0
who? 08	Thomas Edison	978-89-6370-521-7
who? 09	Abraham Lincoln	978-89-6370-522-4
who? 10	Martin Luther King, Jr.	978-89-6370-523-1
who? 11	Louis Braille	978-89-6370-439-5
who? 12	Albert Einstein	978-89-6370-440-1
who? 13	Jane Goodall	978-89-6370-441-8
who? 14	Walt Disney	978-89-6370-442-5
who? 15	Winston Churchill	978-89-6370-443-2
who? 16	Warren Buffett	978-89-6370-444-9
who? 17	Nelson Mandela	978-89-6370-445-6
who? 18	Steve Jobs	978-89-6370-446-3
who? 19	J. K. Rowling	978-89-6370-447-0
who? 20	Jean-Henri Fabre	978-89-6370-448-7
who? 21	Vincent van Gogh	978-89-6370-449-4
who? 22	Marie Curie	978-89-6370-450-0
who? 23	Henry David Thoreau	978-89-6370-451-7
who? 24	Andrew Carnegie	978-89-6370-452-4
who? 25	Coco Chanel	978-89-6370-453-1
who? 26	Charlie Chaplin	978-89-6370-454-8
who? 27	Ho Chi Minh	978-89-6370-455-5
who? 28	Ludwig van Beethoven	978-89-6370-456-2
who? 29	Mao Zedong	978-89-6370-457-9
who? 30	Kim Dae-jung	978-89-6370-458-6